OILS

OILS

Ian Sidaway

This edition first published in 1996 by the
Promotional Reprint Company Ltd,
Kiln House,
210 New Kings Road,
London SW6 4NZ

ISBN 1 85648 376 2

Printed and bound in China

CONTENTS

INTRODUCTION

THE USE OF PIGMENTS, ground and suspended in oil, has been common since the Middle Ages if not earlier, but it was not until the early 15th century that the real potential of the medium began to be recognised, explored and exploited, primarily by the Dutch painter Jan Van Eyck; up until then tempera painting in various forms was used exclusively. The tempera technique imposed certain restrictions on the artist: for a start there was only a limited range of colours and these were difficult to blend; the technique called for a slow building up of form and colour which made it difficult to achieve any degree of naturalism.

Van Eyck dried his varnished tempera paintings done on wooden panels in the sun, as was common practice. When one of these panels split with the heat Van Eyck began to look for a varnish that would dry in the shade. After experimenting he found that linseed and nut oil did just that and soon began to mix his pigments directly into these oils, which he worked in glazes; this gave a brilliance and intensity to his colours that had hitherto not been seen.

After a visit to Flanders Antonello da Messina took Van Eyck's methods back to Venice. At first the Italians were slow in picking up the baton and continued to underpaint in tempera; however, gradually, in the hands of artists such as Giovanni Bellini and Titian, the true strengths and possibilities of oil paint began to be realised. It was also around this time that in Northern Italy - and particularly in Venice - canvas supports began to be used rather than wooden panels.

Today the legacy of these artists along with countless others can be seen hanging on gallery walls throughout the world; more oil paintings hang there than work done in any other medium and in their diversity of technique and style show just how enormously adaptable, versatile and expressive the medium really is.

It is the unmatched depth, intensity and richness of colour that is one of the reasons oil paint is so desirable to use. The wide range of colours that are available and their strength and purity can make colour mixing more straightforward and therefore easier to match those colours seen in the natural world. But perhaps it is the way that oil paint can be adapted to suit the style and approach of an individual that is its biggest strength.

Paint can be applied with brush, knife, fingers, rag or roller, or you can, if you wish, throw it at the support. Paintings can be large and expressive or intimate and small, the paintwork flat and smooth or thick and textured. You can work wet paint over dry paint or wet paint over wet and you can remove and obliterate what you have done by scraping it off with a knife or simply by painting over it. These are just a few of the many ways the paint can be used, yet despite this versatility oil paint is still seen by many to be a difficult medium: in truth it is much easier to work with than watercolour.

This book serves as an introduction to some of the many techniques that are in common practice. After the chapter dealing with equipment and materials you will find a chapter showing the actual techniques, many of which are used throughout the book. It is my belief that practising, experimenting and becoming familiar with these techniques without actually making a picture will help give confidence in handling the materials.

The projects vary in complexity, each one combining techniques with specific picture-making principles. You will be shown how to work wet into wet and wet on dry, how to glaze, when to use a mask and how to paint with a knife, to name but a few. You will also be shown several alternative paintings that deal with and solve similar problems to those illustrated in the project paintings.

As you work remember that making pictures is a subjective process, whilst there are certain principles that need to be acknowledged, these are always open to wide and varied interpretation, and it is this very interpretation that makes for artistic individuality.

MATERIALS AND EQUIPMENT

Canvas boards and other supports

The support is the surface upon which the oil paint sits
or is carried. Oil paint is very obliging in that it will sit
happily on almost anything that has been adequately
and correctly prepared, however certain supports have
a proven record and are far more practical to use than
others. Canvas is synonymous with oil painting and is
the most commonly used support, if not the best.

There are several reasons why this has come
about: canvas is light, making it possible to produce
extremely large paintings that can easily be moved
while still stretched, or if preferred removed from the
stretcher and rolled up. The surface 'give' of stretched
canvas is very responsive to the pressure of the brush,
making it pleasant and comfortable to work on and the
surface tooth or texture takes the paint very easily.
However canvas is but one of many surfaces artists
choose to paint on; together with paper there are many

rigid supports which can also be used and each will
bring a very distinct and different quality to the
finished work.

Various types and weave of canvas can be bought in
a range of sizes. Already stretched and prepared with
either an acrylic or an oil-based primer, these are ready
for painting on, but it is far more economical and satisfying to prepare your own; it is also, as you will see
later, both quick and easy. Canvas that is unprimed
and preprimed is sold by the yard or metre from rolls of
varying width, which can be cut to the required size.
Stretching preprimed canvas can be tricky and as
priming is straightforward it may be best to stick to
unprimed. The thickness of the canvas is described by
ounces per square yard, so the heavier the weight, the
thicker the canvas. In general it is better to use heavier
weight canvas for larger work but anything between
9oz-15oz (25gm-425gm) is good for all round use.

The very best canvas is linen from Belgium, the Netherlands and Ireland. It is made from the decaying stalks of the flax plant, whose seeds also give us linseed oil. The only disadvantage with linen is that it is expensive but in recompense it is extremely strong and almost impossible to tear, with a smooth, closely woven but irregular and unobtrusive weave.

Cotton canvas - also known as cotton duck - is viewed by some as a poor substitute for linen, but it is nevertheless an extremely popular and widely used substitute. Available in a wide range of sizes and weights, cotton duck provides a more than adequate support for your work and it is relatively inexpensive, easy to stretch and almost as tough as linen. The weave of cotton canvas tends to be more regular and mechanical but it is an easy surface to work on and takes the paint well.

Linen and cotton mixtures are also available but are not to be recommended as they both dry to different tensions making them awkward to stretch. Hessian, jute and natural flax can also be used; they have a more open weave and offer, depending on the weight, a coarser surface that is best used for heavy impasto work so that the texture of the weave does not dominate. Synthetic polyester has been used for some time by restorers to reline canvasses, it is very stable and smooth and unlike natural canvas it will never rot. Preprimed polyester canvas can be bought both ready stretched and unstretched and is sure to be used increasingly by artists in the future.

All canvas needs to be stretched over a wooden frame to keep it taut. These wooden stretcher pieces are usually made from kiln-dried, seasoned pine and are bought in pairs that are very slightly bevelled, or raised, on one side so as to keep the canvas proud of the wood. They are already mitred and slotted ready to be joined together and are available in practically any size. Always check for warping by looking along the length of the stretcher bar before buying. Each canvas requires four stretchers and larger canvasses need extra cross pieces to stop them from warping under the considerable tension that a large canvas can exert. Small, triangular wooden wedges can be tapped into the inside of the slotted corners to force them apart and increase the tension once the canvas has been stretched and primed. Stretchers are also available that are round or oval and specialist firms will make up more complex and awkward shapes to order.

Prepared oil painting paper can be bought in a range of sizes and surfaces, as individual sheets or in pads containing several sheets. Whilst not being suitable for work that is considered important and intended for a long permanent life, it is ideal for sketching and preparatory paintings. Most papers can be used if they are substantial enough and adequately sized or primed to protect the paper fibres from the oil. The thicker watercolour papers are especially good as they are heavy enough to stay flat and not cockle when primed and they often have good surface texture. The same is true of ready prepared canvas painting boards made by mounting canvas onto a cardboard backing. These too come in a range of sizes and surfaces and are suitable for smaller works, as well as ideal for sketching and painting on location, but they are prone to bending and warping if they become damp.

Up until the 16th century oils were painted on gessoed wooden panels made mostly from oak, poplar and mahogany. Today with so many modern alternatives available, traditional panels such as these are rarely, if ever, used. Plywood, hardboard (known as masonite in the United States) and the ubiquitous medium density fibreboard (MDF) all offer excellent surfaces to work on, are reasonably priced and can be cut to the desired size. Plywood is made from a variety of woods and in a variety of thicknesses; it is prone to warping so thinner sheets that are of any size need to be reinforced with battens across the back.

The same problem applies to hardboard which has a rough, textured surface, not unlike hessian, on one side and a smooth surface on the other. The smooth surface is usually worked on after being scuffed with a coarse sandpaper to give a little bit of tooth and then primed, but the rougher side can also be used to good effect. MDF is also readily found and is the best of the three. It is also available in a range of thickness but unlike plywood and hardboard is very stable and will not warp, so it does not need battens. Both sides are smooth and can be worked on, but a little extra care should be taken with the corners as they can chip if treated roughly.

Muslin, which is a cheap thin cotton fabric, and scrim, which is also very cheap but is coarser with an open weave, cannot be stretched. However, they can be glued to any of the boards mentioned, by using an acrylic medium to provide a firm, stable and inexpensive alternative to pre-prepared boards. Canvas can also be faced onto MDF in a similar way, with the canvas being secured at the back by staples and an acrylic or PVA adhesive.

Sizing and priming

Whatever the support it will need to be protected and prepared ready to take paint. The oils and chemicals contained in the paint can corrode and deteriorate raw canvas and paper. Most supports are too absorbent to be worked on directly, sucking the oil out of the paint and making it difficult to manipulate. This surface preparation is known as the 'ground'.

\Traditionally the ground is prepared in one of two ways; flexible supports such as canvas are first given a coating of warm glue size which seals and protects the canvas fibres from the corrosive action of the oils and pigments, this also prevents the primer from soaking through. Then a white primer is applied which stays flexible when dry: this fills the weave of the canvas and gives a light reflective surface that takes the paint easily and gives a brilliance to the colours.

Rigid, or non-flexible supports like wood are usually prepared with gesso, which is a mixture of chalk and glue size. The gesso is applied in as many as eight or 10 thin layers; each layer is allowed to dry before the next is brushed on at right angles to the last, the surface can be sanded smooth between coats or after the last coat has been applied and is dry. Traditional gesso is best not used on a flexible canvas support as it may crack.

These traditional proven preparations can still be followed but with the advent of acrylic paint, easy to use prepared acrylic primers and gesso based on polymer resins, all do away with the need for sizing. The acrylic coats the support making it impervious to the corrosive action of oils and driers.

These primers can be thinned with water, dry very quickly and will take to most grease-free surfaces. If grease is a problem, panels can be degreased with methylated spirits. On some linens the first coat sometimes soaks through to the reverse but this can be alleviated by first coating the canvas with an acrylic matte medium thinned with water. Because the primer is acrylic based it enables underpainting and coloured grounds to be made using quick drying acrylic paint. This would not of course be possible if an oil ground was used, because the acrylic will not take to an oil-based primer.

Paint

Oil paint is made by mixing pigment with an extender and a binding medium, usually linseed oil. The paint is available in two basic grades usually referred to as 'student's quality' and 'artist's quality', the distinction between the two is not as pronounced as the difference between student and artist quality watercolour paint. Student quality oil paint from any of the reputable manufacturers is extremely good paint. The difference lies in the higher degree of permanence and durability that is found with most artist's quality colours; these are made from only the finest pigments, use less extender and are very strong and consistent in colour, all of which is of course reflected in their price. So-called student's quality paints are, as stated, very good and are nevertheless used by many professionals; they are often made in a limited range of colours with modern synthetic pigments rather than the more expensive organic and metallic pigments. However, unless you are very familiar with working in oils, you will be hard pressed to detect a difference.

The range of colours available depends on the manufacturer - one Dutch firm has a list of 168. All produce the so-called standard colours with many offering grades of the same colour, and all are intermixable so you do not have to stick to one brand. It may be the case that with time you find that you prefer a blue from one firm or a particular red from another, indeed you may begin to notice that a certain colour from one manufacturer is slightly different from the same colour made by another.

Some paint ranges can be bought by the tin which becomes economical only if you are using considerable quantities. Paint is usually found in tubes ranging from small 8ml tubes increasing in quantity up to 225ml tubes. Some colours, despite rigorous testing and superior manufacturing techniques, are more impermanent and prone to fading than others. The degree of a colour's permanence is indicated on its label, two of the better known manufacturers use a letter and a star system with AA**** meaning extremely permanent colours; A*** durable, considered permanent; B** moderately durable; and C* fugitive.

Pigments vary too, some of them are difficult to manufacture or obtain, and are consequently more expensive than others; so paint is sold in series numbered 1,2,3,4, or, according to manufacturer, A,B,C,D, indicating the price structure, the higher the number or letter the more expensive the paint. Certain pigments are toxic, notably the chromes, the cadmiums and flake white, this too is indicated on the paint label. This will cause no problems whatsoever as long as sensible, straightforward precautions are followed - namely do not eat or drink when using paint and wash before handling food or putting paint-smeared hands on or into your mouth.

Media, solvents and varnish

A medium is added to the paint to change its consistency and texture - making it thin or thick, transparent or opaque or to accelerate its drying time. There are several in both gel and liquid form that are in common use and many more that are less well known made by manufacturers around the world. Some are easily obtainable, some are less easy to find, but all have distinct characteristics and experimentation is by far the best way to find out what those features are and how they can help your style of painting.

The most common and popular medium for oil paint is linseed oil, which thins the paint increasing its transparency. It is to be found in various forms, the best or purest quality oil is cold-pressed, it is also the most expensive. Refined linseed oil is the next best and is more readily available than cold-pressed but it dries more slowly. Sun-thickened and sun-bleached linseed oil are both thicker than other linseeds, they hold brushmarks well and dry much faster. Stand oil is also a linseed derivative, it is an extremely viscous medium that dries to a smooth hard surface with little or no yellowing but it can take some time to dry. Poppy oil is also widely used, it is extracted from poppy seeds and is a pale, slow drying oil that is used with lighter colours. Also available is drying poppy oil which has similar qualities but dries more quickly.

Alkyd media are synthetic resins which have much faster drying times than the naturally extracted oils but actually retain many of their qualities. Liquin is perhaps the best known and has been around for about 40 years; it is clear when mixed with paint making the colour more transparent and it is non-yellowing unlike many of the natural oils. It is excellent for glazing as it dries fast, making a very lengthy operation much shorter. Wingel is thick when first squeezed from the tube but when worked with a palette knife becomes looser and more free flowing, the medium gives body to the paint and is also suitable for building up glazes,

like Liquin it also dries quickly. Oleopasto is a translucent gel that has silica added to make it stiff. It is used specifically for heavy impasto paintwork with a painting knife because it extends the paint yet dries quickly to a strong non-cracking film.

Solvents are essential to oil painting. They dissolve and thin the paint helping it to mix and flow more easily, they then evaporate and have no binding effect whatsoever and because they are clean and clear they have no effect on colour. The best known and most widely used is turpentine, distilled from the oleoresin secreted by pine trees. Turpentine that has been double-rectified to remove the residue of gum, is used for painting, it is as clear as water, but will thicken and discolour if exposed to sunlight and the air so it should be kept in a dark container with an air-tight cap.

White spirit, which is distilled from petroleum oil, is also a powerful solvent; it is cheaper than turpentine and does not yellow but it evaporates faster and more unevenly. It is not recommended for mixing with paint or media but can be used for brush and palette cleaning. For those who are allergic to, or dislike the odour of turpentine and white spirit, low odour thinners are available such as Sansodor or oil of spike lavender. The latter is made by scraping the oily residue from lavender leaves, unlike the other solvents it extends the drying time and is very expensive.

Varnish serves two purposes, it prevents dust and dirt becoming ingrained in the paint surface and it lifts and harmonises the paint work, giving it an even finish. However it is not absolutely necessary or obligatory and often a coat of retouching varnish is all that is needed to restore any sunken areas and perk up the colour. Retouching varnish can be applied over touch dry paint and can even be used between layers of paint. A painting should never be properly varnished until the paint is completely dry, and that can take up to six months, a year or even several years. Varnishes are made from natural resins such as damar, copal and mastic or synthetic resins such as ketone or acrylic: they can all be bought prepared at most art stores.

Brushes

Oil painting brushes are either soft or hard. The soft brushes are made from natural hair or synthetic fibre, the synthetic fibre brushes are more resilient than the natural hair brushes and stand up to the abrasive action of painting with less wear and tear, they are also less expensive. Soft brushes are used for detail, glazing and general finishing work, they deposit the paint flat and smooth with little or no apparent brush mark. Hard or bristle brushes are made from hog's hair and are stiffer and more hard wearing than soft brushes. Bristle brushes can deliver a lot of thick paint to the support and tend to leave their mark in the paint surface making them ideal if you are after expressive and energetic paintwork.

There are five basic brush shapes: rounds, flats, brights, filberts and fan-shaped blenders. The round is the oldest type of painting brush, a versatile all-round brush, capable of making thin or thick lines and flicking in detail. The larger rounds can hold a lot of paint and are superb for laying in broad areas of colour.

The flat is the most adaptable and versatile brush, used for laying-in broad areas of colour and working thick paint in broad confident strokes; when working alla prima and wet into wet, it is also an efficient blender. Used on its edge it can deliver a thin or thick line depending on the pressure. It can also lay paint flat and smooth.

Brights are flat brushes with shorter bristles and so are a lot stiffer and can deliver controlled, precise strokes. They are good for direct impasto work and detail. A filbert is similar to a flat but it has a rounded tip. There are also short filberts that are like a bright, again with a rounded tip. Filberts are rather like well worn flats, they are good for fluid lines and short precise strokes.

The fan blender is just that, a fan-shaped brush that is used for blending together two colours. As the same effect can be achieved with a flat, unless you plan to do a lot of fine blending they are not considered a necessity. A useful addition is a range of decorators' or house painting brushes. They are readily available, are often of very good quality and are cheap and extremely hard wearing: use them for covering large areas and any initial loose, broad blocking in.

Artists' brushes come in series, each series containing the same shape brush in different sizes. As a rule irrespective of the series, oil brushes begin at 001/size 1 the smallest, and increase in size up to 012/size 12 the largest. Decorators' brushes, those used in the home, are sold by the width measurement, ie 25mm (1in), 50mm (2in) and 75mm (3in).

No brush, no matter what it cost, will last and give of its best if it is not looked after, following a few simple rules will keep your brushes in good shape and make them last for a long time. Never leave brushes resting on their points or ends in jars of solvent or thinners; when you have finished using a brush always wipe off excess paint with a rag or paper towel, then rinse it well in a jar of turpentine or white spirit, making sure all the paint has been dissolved from the bristles and from around the ferrule. Next, wash the brush using a washing-up liquid or by gently rubbing the bristles onto a bar of soap, use cold water, rinse the brush clean of soap, gently squeeze the bristles, hair or fibre back to shape and store upright in a pot or jar.

Palette and painting knives

Palette knives are as necessary a piece of equipment as brushes; they are used to mix paint on the palette, to clear up unwanted paint and they can also be used to apply paint and remove unwanted paint from the canvas. Made from steel they come in a wide range of sizes either with a flat blade or a cranked blade which helps keep your knuckles from dipping into the paint. Larger more substantial knives and spatulas with squared-off blades are readily available from DIY and decorating stores.

Painting knives also have a cranked steel blade to keep the hand clear of the painting, the blade is very thin, highly flexible and can be obtained in many different shapes and sizes, round, square, diamond-shaped and oval. Each is capable of producing a range of marks. The technique of painting with a painting knife, oddly enough, is known as palette knife painting.

Palettes

Traditional mahogany kidney-shaped and rectangular palettes are costly, beautiful things that, in line with current thinking, are not especially practical. The problem is the colour, it makes little sense trying to mix a tone or colour on a rich brown surface when you are working on a support that is brilliant white.

However these traditional palettes in mahogany, or cheaper plywood, can be bought in several different sizes as can white faced wooden palettes of similar shape, and rectangular white plastic palettes. Pads of disposable paper - palettes that tear off and can be thrown away once used and dirty - are sold but they are difficult to hold as they are not that substantial and really need to be laid on a flat surface. I work from a large sheet of thick glass that rests on a trolley that can

be manoeuvred close to the easel, It is easy to clean and large enough to allow a lot of colour to be mixed. But whatever you choose to use make sure that it is large enough for your needs and easy to clean.

Easels
You will eventually find that for serious oil painting a good easel really is a necessity. A good easel is practical, holding the canvas firm and steady and at the right height and angle, it is also a help psychologically in that it allows you to work confidently and, silly as it may seem, helps you to feel the part.

There is a large range on the market and the one you choose will depend on what and how you paint. If the space in which you work is limited or you do a lot of painting outdoors on location, then a lighter weight sketching easel would be your best choice. A particularly handy and stable support is the box easel, which consists of a materials and equipment box together with an easel that will hold a medium-sized canvas. The box has a handle for carrying and the whole thing cleverly folds up to the size of a briefcase. A good

studio easel will last you a lifetime and can hold large or small canvasses. These easels are easily tilted and go up and down by means of a ratchet device.

Sundry equipment
The Mahl stick has a long handle with a soft, usually chamois-covered pad at one end; it is used by holding the handle in one hand and resting the pad on the edge of the support or part of the easel. The hand, holding the brush, can then be rested and steadied on the long handle, whilst being kept clear of wet paint.

You will need any amount of jars and containers to mix paint in and hold thinners, but do be careful when using thin plastic yogurt or cream pots as the turpentine and white spirit can dissolve them. Tins are good, as are tin foil containers. Small containers called dippers can be bought to hold linseed oil or other painting media; they clip onto the edge of hand-held palettes. Finally keep a good supply of rags, kitchen paper and newspaper to hand for cleaning your brushes and palettes, mopping up any accidental spills and cleaning your hands.

TECHNIQUES

WHILST IT IS CERTAINLY true that a thorough working knowledge of techniques can liberate the artist to concentrate on the content of his or her work in the sure knowledge that they possess the means to make their vision or idea a two-dimensional reality, it is perhaps surprising to be told that a grasp of technique is of lesser importance when beginning work with oils than when working with any other painting medium.

Oil paint is, despite having a reputation to the contrary, a very easy and forgiving medium to use - unlike watercolour, mistakes are easily and quickly rectified. Furthermore, due to its long drying time alterations, reworking and blending can be done more or less at leisure, unlike acrylic paint which dries so much faster. Oil paint allows the artist great latitude and perhaps the only two rules that need to be put routinely into practice if you want your hard work to last are: thorough preparation of the supports if you are preparing your own, and always work the paint fat over lean.

As you learn about and become familiar with using one technique you will find that it points the way to another and so on, the technique-learning process is cumulative - discovering and becoming familiar with one makes it easier to learn and become familiar with the next. But don't be seduced into believing the painting process will become any easier - you will find that your aspirations will move forward in tandem, tempting you to try your hand at increasingly bigger and better things.

The Techniques

Alla prima is a primary oil painting technique, often referred to as direct painting. The work is executed in one sitting, usually without any drawing or under-painting. The paint is used opaquely and mixed to a smooth buttery consistency. It is applied directly to the support in considered, confident and usually unblended strokes. The correct tones and colours are judged carefully and mixed on the palette; once applied to the support the paintwork is seldom modified. Used correctly the technique gives an exciting fresh paint surface that retains the marks made by the brush or knife and is alive with texture and interest.

Wet into wet painting, whilst having similarities with alla prima, is the technique used when effects, blending, modifications and overworking are carried out into previously applied, but still wet, paint. Oil paint dries slowly so it is not obligatory to complete the painting at one sitting - a painting can be loosely blocked in on location and the work completed later, but before the paint has dried, in the studio. Or perhaps a work painted alla prima on review needs and would benefit from, reworking and alteration. One of the beauties and strengths of oil paint is its capacity for almost unlimited overworking, wet paint can always be scraped off the support with a palette or painting knife. Colours worked into each other in this way blend and mix beautifully but care needs to be taken: too much overworking and the wet paint will lose its fresh look and the colours will become muddy and distinctly lacking in bite.

Paint that is mixed and applied thickly so as to retain the shape of the brush stroke is known as 'impasto', stiff bristle brushes are used to apply the paint in confident direct strokes. The paint is not brushed out onto the support but allowed to sit proud of the surface, giving an almost three-dimensional quality to the work. Adding a gel extender or impasto medium, such as Oleopasto, bulks out the paint and makes it go further without altering the quality or intensity of the colour and without increasing the paint's drying time.

Impasto paint can also be applied with a painting knife; by using a variety of knives it is possible to produce a surprisingly varied range of surface textures.

Painting with a knife is a very tactile occupation and needs to be done well if you are not to end up with a mess. Using up such a quantity of paint, which knife painting inevitably does, requires a sure touch and a little practice. The paint can be floated onto the support, rather like icing a cake, to create a flat surface or dabbed and dotted on using the tip of the knife. By altering the angle of the blade or the direction it is pulled, lines of varying thickness can be made and the knife can further be used to scrape back into the wet paint. It should be remembered that the technique of knife painting need not be employed just by itself but can be used in tandem with other techniques using the brush, rag or even fingers.

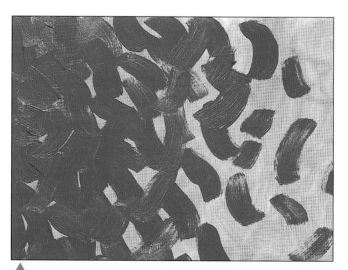

There are few hard and fast rules to follow when painting, but working paint 'fat over lean' is one of the most important ones, standard working practice and should be routinely followed. Paint into which a medium such as linseed, poppy or stand oil is added is referred to as being fat, whilst paint which has been diluted with a thinner such as white spirit or turpentine is known as lean. Lean paint dries at a faster rate than fat paint and should be applied first. Subsequent layers of paint with oil added can then be worked over the top. If the reverse happens, the lean paint dries first, then as the fat paint beneath slowly dries it contracts and can result in the paint surface developing cracks and unsightly wrinkles.

Blending is the merging together of two adjacent colours. It serves to soften the paint edges and can create extremely subtle gradations of colour and tone, allowing forms to be modelled and defined. Blending can be done in several ways and to varying degrees, the long drying time and consistency of oil paint

makes it an ideal medium for the technique. Brushes are the perfect blending tool, with the coarser hog and bristle best used for cruder blending, whilst using the finer synthetics can result in the imperceptible gradation from one colour or tone to another. Flat rather than round brushes should be used as they enable smooth strokes of a consistent pressure to be used to move the paint around. Paint can also be blended using the finger, a rag, the edge of a piece of card or a painting knife.

Sir Henry Tonks, who was the Professor of Painting at the Slade School of Art besides being a fine painter, has the distinction of having a painting technique named after him. 'Tonking' is the deceptively easy and efficient technique of removing excess or unwanted wet paint from the support. By laying a sheet of newspaper over the area of paint to be removed, smoothing it down evenly and then peeling the paper off, the

paint sticks to the absorbent paper and comes away from the support, leaving the area to be reworked, if needed. As well as a means of correcting mistakes the technique can also be used to soften areas of colour after the initial blocking in or underpainting. A variation on the technique, which is useful for smaller, more intricate areas where a thin layer of paint has been used, is the use of masking tape applied and removed in the same way.

'Imprimatura' is the term given to a thin wash or glaze of colour applied to the support to create a coloured ground on which to work. A stark white ground can make tones and colours very difficult to assess in relation with one another. The choice of colour for the imprimatura will depend very much on your subject, any neutral colour can be used but traditionally the choice is an earth colour, green or grey. The colour then acts as a mid tone, making the balancing of the light and dark tones an easier task. The imprimatura will inevitably show through in places, but this is an advantage as it has the effect of harmonising the colours of the painting as a whole.

The wash can be applied with a rag or a large brush using oil paint thinned with white spirit or, if you cannot wait for this to dry, use a thin glaze of acrylic paint mixed with water. Do not worry about getting the glaze flat and even but do make sure it is thin enough to allow the white of the support to glow through as this affects the luminosity and brightness of the colours. Toning the ground achieves pretty much the same effect as an imprimatura but the colour used is opaque and is brushed out evenly over the support.

around the rough surface settling thickly in crevices and lying more thinly on any peaks of paint that are standing proud of the surface.

▲

Glazing is a traditional oil painting technique where thin layers of transparent colours are laid one on top of the other, every layer modifying and altering the one beneath. Each layer is allowed to dry before the next is applied, so the technique can be a slow process and calls for some patience, however the results are quite different from those achieved any other way. The colours, being transparent, allow light to reflect back from the ground, or any opaque underpainting, making the colours mix optically and giving them great depth and richness. Rather than using linseed oil, or turpentine, use a preparatory glazing medium which is easily obtained and will improve the translucency of the paint and speed up the drying process. The technique is especially useful for portrait work when trying to capture those elusive skin tones.

▲

Broken colour is paint that has been applied, usually working wet into wet or alla prima, but without any blending. The colours are applied in small, direct strokes sitting next to each other and, when viewed from a distance, appear to fuse and mix together optically. The Impressionists exploited the technique to the full and it was taken to its extreme in the work of Seurat, Signac and the Pointillists. It can take a little practice to become confident enough to work so directly: keep your colours clean and resist the temptation to 'tickle' and fuss with the paint once it has been applied, because the results give a distinct sparkle and jewel-like quality to the work.

▲

Glazing, like most techniques, does not have to be used by itself but can be effectively combined with others, or it can be used in only one area or section of a painting. It combines especially well with impasto work, the thin transparent colour finds its own way

▲

Scumbling is the application of paint that is usually of a fairly thick and stiff consistency over a previously painted dry layer or the paint can be made thinner to resemble a glaze if you wish. It is then brushed onto the desired area roughly and freely with a stiff bristle brush, finger, sponge or rag in such a way as to allow patches of the underlying colour to show through. Any number of paint layers can be applied in this way as long as each preceding layer is allowed to dry before working on the next; the technique combines well with glazes and is especially valuable for enlivening areas of flat, dull colour.

▲

Masking serves two purposes: firstly it protects areas from becoming covered with unwanted paint or effects and secondly the material used for the mask can introduce a different edge or line quality into the work. Masking tape comes in a wide range of widths, the thinner tapes can be used to create curves whilst the wider tapes can be cut into precise shapes with a sharp scalpel or torn lengthways to give an interesting and unique edge.

▲

For masking out larger areas use paper - either cut or torn. Newspaper will do, but depending on the consistency of the paint it may prove to be too absorbent, allowing the paint to bleed beneath it, spoiling the desired effect. Different papers tear in different ways; I find the best paper is medium weight watercolour

paper so I keep a pile of rejected and failed water-colours that can be torn or cut up just for this purpose. One word of warning, when using a mask work the paint away from the edge so as not to push paint beneath it.

▲

Various other fabrics also make ideal masks and, like paper, they all tear or cut in a different way. Coarse hessians and canvas are especially good as the fibres along the edge tend to unravel giving an interesting, broken line, so if you stretch your own canvas remember to keep those long thin off cuts for this purpose.

▲

Stippling builds up complex textures with thousands of tiny marks and, depending on the size of the area to be covered and the way in which the paint is applied, it can be a lengthy or a reasonably quick process. Stippling can be put to many uses - it can be used to put life into flat areas of paint or it can be built in layers, like glazing, to give a beautiful, subtle, shimmering effect. Stiff decorators' brushes, natural and synthetic sponges, scrubbing brushes, nail brushes, crumpled rags, to name but a few can all be used. Each will make marks that will give a distinct and unique quality to your work.

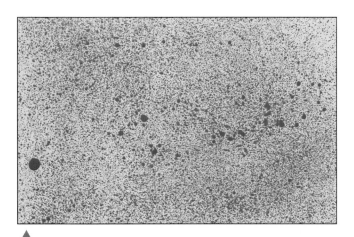

Because it is relatively difficult to control, spattering is usually used together with some form of masking to protect those areas of the painting where the effect is not wanted. Spattering with oil paint can be done in two ways: paint can be spattered onto a dry surface and allowed to dry undisturbed, the resulting spatters will dry with a crisp outline and can be respattered or overworked with another technique. The second way is to spatter onto a layer of wet paint and allow the spattered paint to blend and bleed together with that layer of its own accord. Varying the type and size of brush and the distance it is used from the support surface will produce a range of different effects. Whatever the desired effect it is prudent to experiment on a piece of newspaper first before committing yourself to using the technique on your painting.

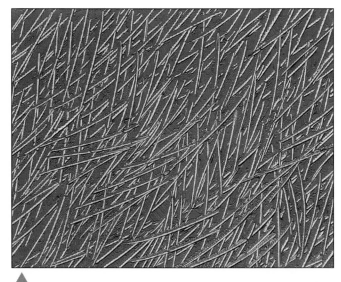

Sgraffito is the technique of scratching through a layer of paint to expose whatever is beneath, which could be the support or another layer of paint. The word comes from the Italian word 'graffiare' which means 'to scratch'. The technique has numerous applications and can produce a wide variety of textural marks; it can be carried out with knives, bits of wood, brush handles, pieces of cardboard and plastic, in fact any implement capable of leaving a mark. Dry paint can be scratched through but a more satisfactory result is achieved when the technique is put to use into wet paint.

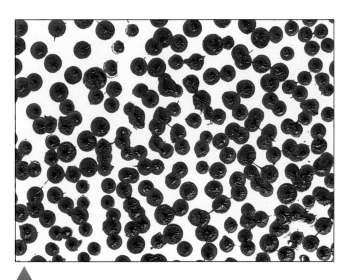

Paint can be used straight from the tube and dotted or smeared onto the support, a technique which can be especially useful to introduce splashes of pure colour and highlights. It is also very effective when used to put in the sparkle on sunlit water.

Ever versatile, oil paint can be mixed with a range of materials such as plaster, sand, sawdust, marble dust and even gravel, to bulk the paint out and create some exciting and uniquely tactile surfaces. Such loaded paint is best applied with a palette knife and can be scratched and worked back into with sgraffito effects or be worked over with other more traditional brush or palette knife techniques.

of the paint and the surface of the support go a long way to deciding how successful the outcome is.

'Frottage' is the technique of rubbing and is normally associated with drawing when paper is laid over a textured surface and a drawing medium is rubbed over that surface so producing an image of the texture lying beneath. It is not possible to do this when working with oils so the technique is practised in reverse. The textured material, be it a coarse fabric, crumpled paper or perhaps bubble wrap, is laid onto the wet paint, gently pressed down and rubbed; those parts that actually come into contact with the surface then take some of the paint away when removed leaving an impression of whatever was used.

Underpainting serves the purpose of providing a firm base or foundation upon which the painting proper can be built. Certain important decisions can be made in the underpainting about the design and composition of the work and the distribution of tone and colour. This preliminary painting can be done broadly and loosely using thin paint and colours that approximate those colours to be used in the final painting. A more traditional approach is to start with a tonal underpainting using only one colour. This monochromatic underpainting establishes the tonal values and can be done in any colour that is sympathetic to the overall colour of the subject, but like the colours used when laying an imprimatura, earth colours, terra verte or grey, are traditional and proven.

Imprinting, when used with oils, is in many ways similar to frottage and the two techniques are interchangeable, being different in name only. Here I have painted a leaf and simply printed it by pressing it onto the surface of a sheet of oil painting paper, but any flat, natural or man-made object can be treated in much the same way. As with frottage the consistency

Paint can be applied in any number of ways and you should not feel restricted to using just the brush or the knife. A crumpled piece of rag can lay colour down very quickly and broadly and is an excellent tool for blocking in as it forces a broader view that precludes becoming involved with details at too early a stage.

STRETCHING CANVAS

ALL CANVAS NEEDS to be stretched taught and prepared with a ground to seal and protect it before it can be painted on. Pre-stretched, prepared canvas can be bought in a range of popular sizes but they are expensive. Stretching your own is quick and straight-forward, satisfying and very economical, stretchers can be reused time and again simply by taking off paintings that you are unhappy with and restretching them with fresh canvas.

Whilst the procedure is the same for all canvas, be it fine linen, cotton duck or hessian, you will find that each type of canvas stretches in a slightly different way. Medium weight cotton duck is very easy, it just needs to be pulled flat and reasonably taut, the size or acrylic primer does all of the work. Once sized or primed the wet canvas fibres shrink as they dry, pulling themselves tight over the stretcher.

Linen dries and stretches tauter than cotton so care must be taken not to pull it too tight prior to priming, after which it will tighten like a drum. When using linen it is better to position the warp thread of the canvas across the shortest distance; the warp thread is the thread that runs the entire length of a roll of canvas.

Rather than using your fingers to pull the canvas tight you may find it easier to use straining pliers, but again, take care not to pull the canvas over-tight before it has been primed.

The Techniques

You will need four stretcher pieces of the required length and eight wooden or plastic wedges, a length of canvas, a pair of scissors, a tape measure, a staple gun with rust-proof staples and a hammer.

Assemble the stretcher frame by slotting the four pieces together, making sure that they all have the bevelled edge on the same side. The stretchers should slide into each other easily, if not gently tap them home with a wooden mallet or hammer. If you use a hammer use a wooden block between it and the stretcher to protect the stretcher edge from becoming dented. Once assembled measure from corner to corner both ways and when the measurements are the same the stretcher will be square. If you do not have a tape measure improvise using a piece of string.

Place the assembled stretcher, bevel side down, on a piece of canvas. Make sure that the weave of the canvas runs parallel with the stretcher frame and then carefully cut the canvas leaving an overlap of 2-3in (5-7cm) around all the edges.

Once you have reached the corners place the stretcher canvas side down and staple the canvas to the back of the stretcher, fixing the staples roughly half-way between those on the edge. At the corner fold the canvas corner point over the edge and back of the stretcher, so that it points toward the middle of the canvas .

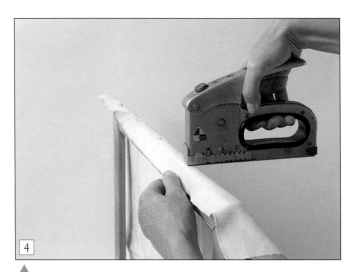

Fold the canvas up and over the back of one side and secure it to the frame edge with one staple placed in the centre of the stretcher. On the opposite stretcher pull the canvas taught and place another staple in the same position. Do the same on the other two sides. Now add a staple about 6in (15cm) on either side of the centre staple and the same on the opposite side pulling the canvas taught; do the same on the other two sides. Once a staple is in, always pull the canvas taught before securing its opposite number. The amount of staples you need along each edge depends on the size of the stretcher but as a general rule fix a staple every 4-6in (10-15cm).

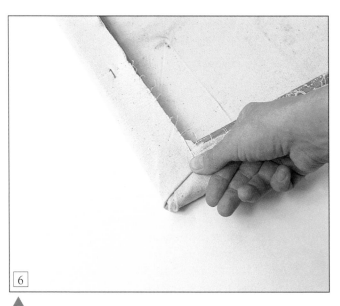

Fold the two flaps in, one on top of the other and secure them with a staple.

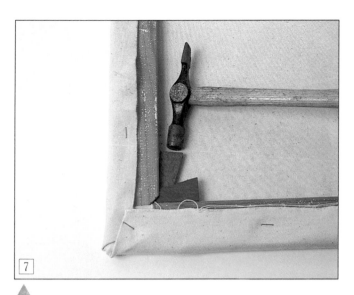

Tap the wedges gently into the slots inside each corner, being careful not to force the corners apart and tighten the canvas.

The canvas is then ready to be sized and primed traditionally or, as here, given two coats of acrylic primer. Once dry the canvas should be nice and taut but if there is any slack it can be taken up by knocking the wedges firmly into the corners - this is known as wedging out. It is useful to know that canvas tightens and stretches more when traditional size and primer is used and it stretches a little less taught when acrylic primers are used. This should be taken into serious consideration when you are pulling the canvas over the stretcher prior to stapling.

COLOUR

The primary colours - red, yellow and blue - cannot be mixed from other colours, hence their name. Red and yellow make orange, yellow and blue, green, and blue and red make purple or violet: these are known as secondaries. But as a casual glance at a paint colour chart will show there are many different reds, yellows and blues and the secondary colours obtained will depend very much on which of these primaries are used. The same is true of the tertiary colours - these are the colours that fall between the primaries and the secondaries. They are made up by mixing an equal amount of a primary colour with an equal amount of the secondary next to it, to obtain a red-orange, orange-yellow, yellow-green, green-blue, blue-violet and violet-red.

All colours are considered to be either warm or cool; the warm colours are red, orange and yellow, the cool colours are green, blue and violet. However the terms 'warm' and 'cool' are relative as all colours have a warm and cool variant. There are warm reds, such as cadmium, which have a yellow bias, and cool reds, like alizarin crimson, which have a blue bias. To confuse the issue further, a colour that is seen as warm in isolation can appear cool when seen next to a warmer variant of a similar colour. This warm/cool colour relationship is very important and can be put to good use, especially when you are painting the landscape, as warm colours seem to advance visually towards the viewer and cool colours appear to recede.

When mixing colours bear in mind that a more intense, brighter third colour will result if mixed from two colours that have a bias toward each other. For example, cadmium red (yellow bias) and cadmium yellow (red bias) create a bright, vivid orange, whereas alizarin crimson (blue bias) and cadmium yellow (red bias) mix to create a more subdued, less intense orange. This is because alizarin crimson is closer to yellow's complementary colour, violet.

Complementary colours are those colours that fall opposite one another on the colour wheel. One colour will always have a warm bias, the other will have a cool bias. Hence red is the complementary of green and orange is the complementary of blue; these colour opposites are known as complementary pairs and have a very special relationship. When placed next to each other complementary pairs have the effect of enhancing or intensifying each other. However, if you mix a small amount of a colour into its complementary, the colour will be subdued, or knocked back. Add more of a colour's complementary colour and you will neutralise it completely, producing a range of neutral greys and browns. It is important to be able to mix and exploit these less vivid, subdued colours as they echo many of the colours seen in nature and help bring an overall harmony to the work.

Colour is a complex and intriguing subject and a basic knowledge of the theory is certainly necessary, but the very best way to understanding what is possible and why, is to spend time experimenting with your colours. But do remember to make notes, the combinations using just a few colours are countless and the chances of mixing a colour and immediately forgetting how you did it is a real possibility.

Choosing Colours

There are many colours to choose from, - one manufacturer offers 168 variants and it is, of course, neither economically viable or practical to work with anywhere near this many. Most professional artists use only a limited range of colours having learnt from experience the mixtures these are capable of producing. I regularly use 18 different colours plus white, but seldom do I use them all together in one painting and some are used out of convenience simply to save mixing. The colours I use are listed below, those marked with an * I suggest are an ideal choice for a starter palette which, should you feel the need, can be added to and extended at a later date.

TITANIUM WHITE: * is a very bright clean white, it is very opaque so you will need only a small amount to lighten a colour. It dries slowly but this can be speeded up with the addition of dryers.

PAYNE'S GREY: * a cool grey that is useful to knock back or modify colours without destroying their brilliance. It also makes, when mixed with burnt or raw umber, a good black.

RAW UMBER: * is a versatile colour that, like Payne's grey, can be used to tone down more strident colours. It is a useful colour for underpainting and dries quickly.

BURNT UMBER: is a rich, warm, strong brown that mixes well with other colours, especially green, and like raw umber it dries very quickly.

RAW SIENNA: is a semi-transparent colour that when used thinly is a bright yellow. It mixes well with most colours and dries fairly quickly.

BURNT SIENNA: * is a powerful, bright, red brown that needs to be used with caution. It dries reasonably quickly and is a good choice when mixing flesh tones and also for glazing.

YELLOW OCHRE: * a similar colour to raw sienna and with some makes of paint it can be difficult to tell them apart. Yellow ochre dries more slowly than sienna but is more opaque and extremely useful for mixing flesh tones.

NAPLES YELLOW: is a useful addition to the portrait painter's palette, it dries fairly quickly and is opaque.

CADMIUM YELLOW: * is a strong, slow-drying yellow that is available in light, medium and dark tones. It mixes well with blues and reds to make a range of bright greens and oranges.

LEMON YELLOW: * is a cool yellow that, like cadmium yellow, mixes well to make a range of oranges and greens.

CADMIUM ORANGE: can be mixed from cadmium red and cadmium yellow. I use it out of convenience.

CADMIUM RED: * a strong, warm, slow-drying red that is available in light and dark versions, it mixes well with greens to make a range of browns and is invaluable to the portrait painter.

ALIZARIN CRIMSON: * a cool, transparent and slow-drying red, again useful to the portrait painter and capable of mixing with the blues to create a range of purples and violets.

ULTRAMARINE: * is a strong, warm, transparent blue that dries slowly, it mixes well with alizarin crimson and the yellows.

COBALT BLUE: * is a cool, transparent, fast-drying blue

useful for glazes, portrait work and subtle blue skies.

CERULEAN BLUE: a fairly weak, semi-transparent blue that is useful for skies and modifying other colours.

MONESTIAL OR PTHALOCYANINE BLUE: is one of the strongest blues and needs to be used with care, it is transparent and dries slowly:

VIRIDIAN: * is possibly the only premixed green that is really needed. It is a transparent, slow-drying green that mixes well with reds, yellows and browns to create a wide range of greens.

SAP GREEN: is a bright easily-modified green useful for landscape painting

Colour Theory – The Basics

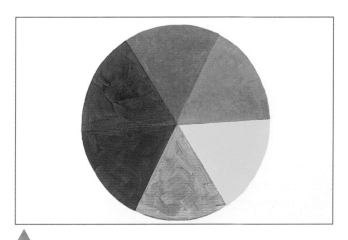

▲
This colour wheel is mixed using 'warm' primaries, cadmium red, cadmium yellow and ultramarine.

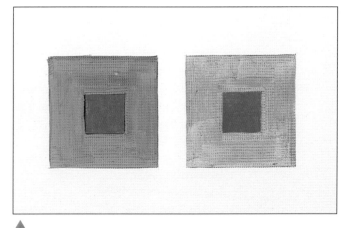

▲
A colour is noticeably affected by the colour that is next to it. Here the red square seems to be much brighter when surrounded by its complementary green.

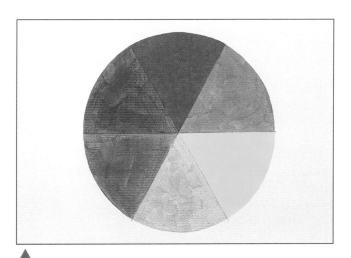

▲
Here the secondaries have been mixed using the 'cool' primaries, alizarin crimson, lemon yellow and cerulean blue.

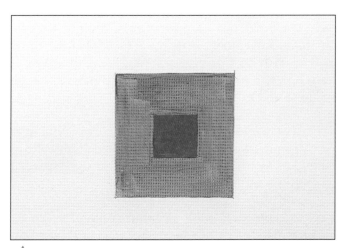

▲
Warm colours will seem to advance and cool colours recede.

All colours have an equivalent corresponding grey tone on a scale that runs from black through to white.

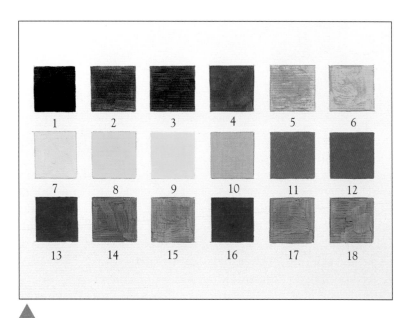

My palette of colours.

1 Payne's grey	7 Naples yellow	13 Ultramarine
2 Raw umber	8 Cadmium yellow	14 Cobalt blue
3 Burnt umber	9 Lemon yellow	15 Cerulean blue
4 Burnt sienna	10 Cadmium orange	16 Monestial blue
5 Raw sienna	11 Cadmium red	17 Virdian
6 Yellow ochre	12 Alizarin crimson	18 Sap green

IN THE ALCAZAR SEVILLE

Alla Prima

PROJECT ONE

ALLA PRIMA IS ONE OF the primary oil painting techniques. Translated from the Italian it means 'at the first' and is used to describe paintings that are executed at a single sitting or in one 'wet'.

This direct method of painting is the style that found favour with the Impressionists who, with the invention of the collapsible paint tube in 1841, found it possible to work easily away from the studio en plein air. Working from nature in this way meant that the working practice of artists had to change, they needed to work faster in order to catch the ever-changing light and changes in the weather. Artists, with a few exceptions, had until then worked in the studio where it was possible to build a work slowly with layers of scumbles and glazes.

Regardless of whether you are working outside or in, it is important not to set yourself an impossible task, in other words make sure that you can finish the painting in the time that you have available. This means choosing your subject sensibly and working on a support that is not too large. Working in this way means you should only need a minimum of equipment one, two or three brushes at the most, a few tubes of carefully chosen paint, a support, an easel and turpentine and, if you wish, an oil medium such as Liquin or linseed oil.

Try to work with direct confident brush strokes laying colours and tones next to each other on the support, gradually building up something that resembles a mosaic. Mix the paint to a buttery consistency so that it leaves the brush easily, but is not so thin as to run, and try not to go over work already done, one of the attractions of alla prima work is its immediacy and spontaneity.

This view of a square, which is part of the magnificent Alcazar in Seville, was a good subject. A compositional balance is created by the row of trees, doors and windows at the top and the dark shadow of the orange tree in the foreground, which on a practical level made a relatively cool place to sit!

This painting was done on a prepared canvas board that measured 18x12in (45.5x30.5cm). I used a stick of charcoal for the underdrawing, a no4 flat bristle brush, and Payne's grey, raw umber, ultramarine, yellow ochre, cadmium red, viridian, lemon yellow, monestial blue and titanium white oil paint, Liquin and turpentine.

MATERIALS AND EQUIPMENT

Stick of charcoal
no4 flat bristle brush
Payne's grey, raw umber, ultramarine, yellow ochre, cadmium red, viridian, lemon yellow, monestial blue, titanium white

The Painting

1 Using a piece of medium charcoal, a loose drawing quickly establishes the composition. Pay particular attention to any vertical and horizontal lines and make sure they run true. Finally draw in the orange tree at an angle and its shadow cast in the foreground.

2 Dust off any excess charcoal with a large brush or by flicking over the surface with a soft, clean rag. With a no4 flat bristle brush mix Payne's grey and raw umber and paint in the dark leaves at the top of the picture, the dark shadows in the line of trees and the trunk of the tree in the foreground. Do not make the paint too loose, keep it to a buttery consistency.

3 Into this dark mixture add some ultramarine blue and yellow ochre together with a little titanium white. Block in the dark shadows cast by the leaves in the foreground and the shadows from the line of trees seen in the distance.

4 Using the same mix, paint in the doorways behind the row of trees and the dark line that runs across the top of the building. Add a little raw umber, yellow ochre and white and complete blocking in the trunk of the foreground tree. Cadmium red and yellow ochre, together with a little of the previous mix and some white, give a dark brown for the stonework around the fountain and at the base of the post standing in the centre of the square.

5 A mid-green is mixed with viridian, lemon yellow and a little raw umber, some of this is lightened with white and lemon yellow and some made darker by adding raw umber and Payne's grey. The trees are then painted with these three mixtures using sure strokes to describe the shape of the foliage.

6 Yellow ochre and cadmium red together with a little raw umber make the dull orange that can be seen surrounding the doors and windows. The blue-grey band at the base of the building is painted with a mix of Payne's grey and titanium white; ultramarine is added for the shadow beneath the dark parapet and at the base of the post.

7 A light blue mixed from monestial blue and titanium white establishes the small bit of sky. Attention is now turned to the fountain where a cadmium red, yellow ochre, white and a little grey mix gives the colour for the stonework.

8 Cadmium red, yellow ochre and titanium white give the light sand colour seen on the ground, with this mix work carefully down the painting cutting in and around any paintwork already done.

9 As the foreground work is approached, darken the mix a little by adding more yellow ochre and cadmium red and paint around the shadow of the tree. Keep plenty of paint on the brush and dab in the dappled light.

10 Pure titanium white straight from the tube is then used for the stark facade of the building, it is worked carefully around the doors, windows and trees.

11 Finally a few highlights are indicated on the lamp post and a few touches of a lighter green in the trees complete the picture.

Alternative Approaches

1 This small painting of anemones was painted in a couple of hours. A fairly precise drawing helped keep the painting on track. Only two or three tones have been used for each colour, but the forms still read convincingly.

2 This early morning view in Venice looking from St Marks Square across to San Giorgio Maggiore was painted with a limited palette consisting of four colours: white, Payne's grey, cerulean blue and raw umber.

SKULL AND POTS

Tonal Underpainting

MONOCHROME underpainting allows you to concentrate on all the tones without becoming absorbed in, and confused by, the colour - think of it as a black and white snapshot rather than a colour photograph.

A grey underpainting is the starting point for the traditional technique of glazing, and is known as a grisaille. Once this grey underpainting is dry the colours can be glazed over it in transparent layers. However an underpainting can be helpful even if you intend not to work with glazes establishing, as it does, the overall composition and tonal range and giving you the opportunity to make alterations and corrections before beginning the work proper. It also serves to get rid of the intimidating stark white ground.

The underpainting can be in any colour that is sympathetic to the subject, traditionally the colours chosen are neutral earth colours, or terre verte - a dull green. Here we have used raw umber mixed with a little Payne's grey. When underpainting in oils, thin the paint with turpentine to keep it lean; you may need to wait a few hours or even over night before this is dry enough to work on top of, alternatively use acrylic paint which will dry in a few minutes.

Still life painting, regardless of the actual objects used, is a marvellous way to learn about some of the primary principles of art. The objects being of a manageable size can be manipulated and moved around into different groupings, showing variations of composition, perspective and colour. Anything can be used, you don't have to look far as every home is full of subjects, from kitchen utensils to childrens' toys. Here I have used a few glazed pots, a wooden box, a wooden ball and a skull, all are similar in tone making the choice of colour used for the underpainting an easy one, matching, as it does, the local colour or actual colours of many of the objects.

The painting was done on a primed cotton duck canvas measuring 18x24in (45.5x61cm)using titanium white, Payne's grey, raw umber, raw sienna, burnt sienna, yellow ochre, cadmium orange and cadmium red, diluted and thinned with Liquin and turpentine. The paint is applied with ¼in and ½in (6mm and 12mm) flat synthetic brushes and a no4 and a no8 flat bristle. A thin stick of medium charcoal was used for the underdrawing.

MATERIALS AND EQUIPMENT

6mm/12mm flats, no4 and 8 bristle brushes
stick of medium charcoal
titanium white, Payne's grey, raw umber, raw sienna, burnt sienna, yellow ochre, cadmium orange and red

The Painting

1 With a thin piece of charcoal draw in and position the objects. Work carefully and try to position things correctly in relation to each other. A few measurements may help. When drawing in the objects indicate the direction and fall of any shadows. Once the drawing is complete remove any excess charcoal by dusting over the canvas with a soft brush or a clean rag. Then give the drawing a coat of fixative.

2 The monochromatic, or tonal underpainting is done in a mix of raw umber and Payne's grey acrylic paint which dries in minutes. Oil paint thinned with turpentine would need to dry for several hours or over night before work on the overpainting could begin. The light mid tone is established first using a flat ½in (12mm) synthetic brush.

3 Gradually, in careful stages, the darker tones are searched out and established and the form of the objects begins to be progressively apparent.

4 Once dry begin working across the painting with a ¼in (6mm) flat brush using oils mixed with turpentine and Liquin. Starting with the Moroccan jar on the left using burnt umber, yellow ochre and a little white, the darks are painted. The mix is lightened a little for the patches of mid tone with cadmium orange, white and a little cadmium red; this brown is also seen on the wooden ball. The mix is lightened further with white and the jar blocked in.

5 Cadmium red is added to the mix and the red glaze inside the large pot on the right is established using a no8 flat bristle. The same mix is brushed over the side of the wooden box, the wooden ball and the side of the large pot.

6 Raw umber darkens the mix and using the ¼in (6mm) flat the dark beneath the rims of the jars and the shadow on the large jar thrown by the skull are painted in. Also the shadow on the front of the box and the dark wood on the ball are blocked in.

7 Yellow ochre and raw sienna together with the previous mix and some white give a range of colours and tones for the large pot. A few reflections are flicked in to help suggest the gloss of the glaze. The same yellow mix is used, thinned well with turps, for the base colour seen on the tabletop. The large areas of colour are blocked in with the no4 flat and the detail and finer shapes with the ¼in (6mm) flat, brush a little of this colour over the skull.

8 Raw umber deadens the yellow mix used for the jug and gives the basic mixture used on the skull. Payne's grey and raw umber are mixed for the shadows and white is added to the basic mixture for the highlights. Some of this mixture is pulled down and used to block in the small, light pot on the left. All detail and work in confined areas is done with the ¼in (6mm) soft brush and all the blocking of larger areas with the no4 flat.

9 The small light pot is blocked in with white, Payne's grey and a little raw umber. Burnt sienna, raw umber and cadmium red give a mix for the wooden box and the tops of the two jars on the right. Again all the details are painted with the ¼in (6mm) flat and more open blocking in with the no4 flat bristle.

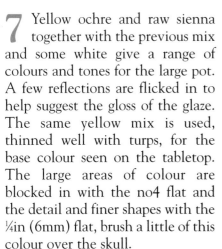

10 The bodies of the two pots are painted next with raw umber, yellow ochre and titanium white. The shadows on the table are darkened and the background pale colour is blocked in using the no8 flat bristle brush using titanium white with a little raw umber and Payne's grey. The painting is then allowed to dry over night.

11 Once dry start to rework the painting, begin by strengthening the darks and lightening the lights in an effort to stretch the tonal range.

12 The painting is completed by reworking the tabletop and repainting the background with titanium white mixed with a little raw umber.

Alternative Approaches

1 This painting of a hillside in Tuscany was painted in much the same way as the main project, the shape, position and tone of the fields and trees all being established using thin washes of a dull purple.

2 The overall colour of this painting of a boatman waiting for custom suggested that the underpainting should be done with a mixture of ochre and grey. The underpainting can still be seen in the light reflections on the water and around the steps and paving.

GARDENING TOOLS

Underdrawing and Underpainting

PROJECT THREE

AS MENTIONED in the previous project the stark white of a support can be very intim-idating, making it very difficult to make those first few marks on the canvas - covering it quickly with a drawing or underpainting commits you and helps you to relax into it, but it also provides a good solid foundation for the work to come.

An underdrawing can be made using pen and ink, coloured pencils, pastel, conte crayon, indeed most drawing media except felt tip and marker pens as the ink in these tends to bleed through the subsequent layers of paint. But perhaps the medium that is most commonly used for the purpose is charcoal; this takes very easily to most surfaces, its very nature encourages a bold, fluid line that forces you to concentrate on the image as a whole rather than in detail and mistakes are easily dusted away with a cloth or a large soft brush.

Once all the drawing is in place to act as a guide, a loose underpainting will help to consolidate the composition. The idea is to work broadly and directly, establishing the overall local colours, again ignoring any detail; to this end choose either large brushes or soft rags. Remember the 'fat over lean' rule and mix the paint with turpentine only. This mixture should be thin enough to allow overworking almost immediately as the turpentine evaporates from the paint quite quickly leaving a thin, tacky film of colour that will take thicker paint easily.

Again a group of objects make up a still life, but this time the garden shed was the source. After playing around with the composition it was decided to look almost straight down on the group. Allowing a couple of the pots to run off the top of the picture adds tension and makes for a more interesting composition, the eye wants to travel out of the picture to see what is there, but is pulled back in by the circular grouping of the other objects.

It was painted on a 20x30in (51x76cm) pre-prepared canvas board using a thick stick of charcoal for the drawing, a rag for the underpainting and a single no4 flat bristle brush. The colours used were titanium white, Payne's grey, raw umber, burnt umber, burnt sienna, yellow ochre, cadmium yellow, lemon yellow, cadmium red, cadmium orange, alizarin crimson, viridian and sap green. The paint was thinned and mixed with turpentine and linseed oil.

MATERIALS AND EQUIPMENT

no4 flat bristle brush
stick of charcoal
titanium white, Payne's grey, raw umber, burnt sienna, yellow ochre, cadmium yellow, red and orange, lemon yellow, alizarin crimson, viridian, sap green

The Painting

1 With a large thick piece of charcoal loosely draw in the pots, trug basket and tools, and scribble in the darker areas of shadow. If you wish this can be dusted over or given a coat of spray fixative, either way the drawing will disappear beneath the layers of paint.

2 With burnt sienna thinned with turpentine and using a small piece of rag, paint in the overall colour of the flowerpots. Using the rag lays colour in quickly and makes it impossible to focus on detail. With raw umber do the same to the trug basket and with cadmium yellow and lemon yellow paint in the gloves. A little viridian and cadmium red is used for the seed packets.

3 Mix yellow ochre and titanium white and block in all of the background, work quickly and don't be afraid of smudging what has been done or straying over lines, the intention is simply to cover the area quickly.

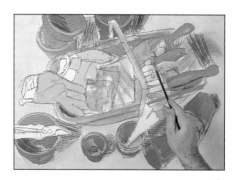

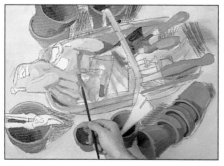

4 In the time it takes to make and drink a cup of coffee much of the turpentine will have evaporated and the thin paint will have taken on a stiffer, greasy appearance ready to be overpainted. With a no4 flat bristle begin to block in the local (actual) colour of the objects. Begin with the flowerpots using a mixture of burnt sienna, cadmium orange, yellow ochre and titanium white. Ochre, white and raw umber mixes give the colour for the handles of the tools.

5 Some of the flowerpot mixture is darkened with burnt umber and Payne's grey and the dark tones inside and between the flowerpots painted. A little sap green and white give the colour for the trowel and the gloves are worked with cadmium orange, lemon yellow, burnt sienna and white.

6 Sap green and yellow ochre with a little white give the mix for the seed packets. Then the shadows are scrubbed in using a combination of darker mixes made from the dark colour used for the inside of the flowerpots with ochre and white added.

7 Payne's grey and burnt umber give a dark that is used for the shadows around the objects, the dark wood around the trug basket and the handle. Cadmium orange is used on the garden line and a dark mix of cadmium red, alizarin crimson and the dark shadow mix gives the colour for the handle of the secateurs. The dark red is lightened by the addition of more cadmium red and the radishes, illustrated on the seed packet, are blocked in.

8 Next the trug is reworked using raw umber, yellow ochre and white with a little cadmium red added. The picture on the seed packets is developed and the dark blade of the secateurs and the edge of the gloves blocked in.

9 Gradually detail is added and the secateurs and trug basket are completed, also the coloured pattern that runs around the wrist of the gloves is painted. Highlights on the edge of the pots are dabbed in and pure white is used for the plant labels and the highlights on the garden tools.

10 Neutral greys are mixed by combining red, yellow ochre and Payne's grey together with a little raw umber and white, these are used for the shadows that run across the background cloth

11 Finally yellow ochre and white are added to the above and the background is reworked cutting in and around the objects, giving them a crisp outline.

Alternative Approaches

1 The entire surface of this small painting of a young woman swimming was loosely washed over with various tones of blue using a large decorating brush. Once this had dried the painting was completed.

2 The underpainting of this small painting of the model boats that are for hire in the Luxembourg Gardens in Paris was done quickly on the spot using acrylic paint. The picture was then completely reworked in oil paint in the studio several weeks later.

THE CLIFFS AT ETRETAT

Thin Paint

PROJECT FOUR

THIN PAINT that is mixed with a dryer such as Liquin is slightly transparent and can be the ideal medium for blocking in and establishing a scene on location; the painting can then be reworked later in the studio at leisure. Often after only a few hours the painting will be dry enough to begin overpainting, again using thin paint mixed with a dryer. The technique is not dissimilar to glazing, as elements of the underpainting are allowed to show through and influence the next layer of paint.

In many respects this technique is not unlike those used in traditional watercolour work. For the most part, like watercolour, the painting is worked light to dark, colours are strengthened and darkened in the reworking whilst the lightest areas of colour and tone are left unpainted, having been established in the initial underpainting. The white of the canvas reflecting through the semi-transparent layers lights the paintwork from within and even acts as the white surf and foam in the sea. The textures seen on the cliffs and in the foaming sea are represented solely by the effects of flat paint work, there is no impasto or thick paint used.

Landscape as a subject is as vast and infinitely variable as the landscape itself. The view from your kitchen window is as legitimate a subject as sunflower fields in Italy, or an Arizona desert studded with cactus. It is even possible, as so many artists have done in the past, to paint the same view over and over again, changing as it will in different weather conditions, times of day or seasons of the year. You should not need to look far for inspiration. However, whatever, or whenever you decide to paint, try to look at your subject in a fresh and original way. This is often easier said than done or certainly easier with some places than with others. Venice, for instance, must surely have been the inspiration for more paintings than any other city in the world, yet artists, including myself, still flock there to work in an effort to create something that is fresh and original.

This view looking down from the cliffs at Etretat in Normandy was painted on a 19x22in (48x59cm) primed cotton duck canvas using charcoal for the underdrawing, a no4 and a no8 flat bristle brush and a ¼in (6mm) flat synthetic brush. The colours used were titanium white, Payne's grey, raw umber, burnt umber, raw sienna, cadmium yellow, lemon yellow, cadmium red, ultramarine, cerulean blue and sap green, the paint was thinned with turpentine and Liquin.

MATERIALS AND EQUIPMENT

6mm flat/ no4 and 8 bristle brushes titanium white, Payne's grey, raw umber, burnt umber, raw sienna, cadmium yellow and red, lemon yellow, ultramarine, cerulean blue, sap green

The Painting

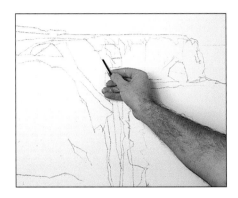

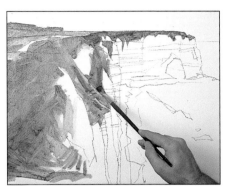

1 With a medium stick of charcoal loosely and lightly sketch in the cliffs and the beach. Fix well afterwards with a spray fixative.

2 With a mix of sap green and cadmium yellow thinned with turpentine and Liquin, and using the no4 and no8 flat brushes, block in the light, grassy areas on the cliff top. Darken the mix with Payne's grey and burnt umber and establish the darker greens along the cliff edge.

3 Payne's grey, burnt umber and white mixes are used to establish the general colour of the cliffs and the shingle beach.

4 With cerulean blue, titanium white and a little lemon yellow and using the no 8 flat brush block in the sky, the mixture is lightened a little at the horizon helping create the illusion of aerial perspective.

5 Darken the sky mix with ultramarine and lemon yellow and paint in the sea, darken this mix further with Payne's grey and more ultramarine for the shadow below the cliffs that crop out into the sea.

6 Once the paint has dried, (this should take just a few hours or at the most over night) work can be resumed. With a ¼in (6mm) flat synthetic brush and sap green darkened with a little raw umber, darken and consolidate the grass that is in shadow and the row of windswept trees on the horizon.

7 Still using the ¼in (6mm) brush and a mix of raw umber and raw sienna, the patch of eroded earth in the centre of the cliffs is darkened. Payne's grey together with a little titanium white and cerulean blue is used next to paint the strata on the rocky outcrop.

8 Add a little raw sienna to the mix and continue to suggest the rock strata on the cliffs that run parallel to the sea.

9 Burnt sienna, cadmium red, Payne's grey and white give the colour for the beach. The green on the nearest cliff top is then darkened with sap green, raw umber and Payne's grey using the no8 flat brush. Also darken the shadow beneath the row of trees but using the ¼in (6mm) flat.

10 Payne's grey, sap green and a little cerulean blue are mixed for the shadow on the sea below the cliffs. The mix is lightened with more cerulean blue, payne's grey and a little titanium white and the dark patterns on the sea blocked in with the ¼in (6mm) flat.

11 The sky is painted using the no8 flat bristle brush with a light cerulean blue, lemon yellow and titanium white mix. Darken the mix with a little more blue and yellow and paint in the wave patterns on the sea using the ¼in (6mm) soft brush.

12 Again using the no8 flat consolidate the light sea colour with a mixture made from cerulean blue, lemon yellow and white together with a little Payne's grey.

13 Finally pure white is used with the no8 flat along the shore line to soften the edge of the surf.

Alternative Approaches

1 Very thin mixes of colour diluted with turpentine were used on a smooth canvas board for this working study of the Sphinx at Giza in Egypt. The paint was scrubbed on in layers and allowed to run in places, all in an attempt to suggest the texture of corroded stone and sand.

2 Using a photograph as reference, this painting of my daughter was also done using thin paint built up in layers, each layer being allowed to dry before the next was painted. This can be seen in the reflection where the colours and tones overlap each other like glazes.

WHITE LILIES

Mixing Techniques

CERTAIN TECHNIQUES bring a very distinct quality to a work, they can be used by themselves to create a complete painting or, as is more often the case, introduced to resolve a representational problem, and in doing so they often bring a very different and interesting quality to the paint surface. One of these techniques is masking. Masking prevents certain areas of a painting from being covered in paint and in doing so can, depending on the material used, create a very distinct edge that is impossible to achieve in any other way.

Masks can be made from any material that can be laid flat onto the work and fixed to prevent paint from seeping beneath it. The most commonly used materials are masking tape, paper or card and fabric; however masking is one of those areas that calls for experimentation and what you use will depend very much on the desired result. Masking tape is used to mask out small areas of a painting but because it needs to stick to the surface the paint needs to be dry. The tape can be torn and then applied or cut into intricate shapes with a sharp scalpel once it has been laid, care must be taken

not to press so hard that you cut through the support as well as the tape. Paper can also be cut and torn creating either a smooth or ragged edge. Paper can be used on wet paint as it only rests on the surface, the same goes for fabrics. However the consistency of the paint is very important: if it is too thin you will find that it creeps and bleeds beneath the mask spoiling the effect, very thick paint can be used with either a brush or painting knife and if used with a thick mount, like card, makes an edge that stands proud of the surface in the same way as impasto paintwork.

Sgraffito is a traditional technique that, like masking, is usually used to bring qualities to the paint work that would be difficult, if not impossible, to achieve in any other way. Scratching through the wet paint can enliven a dead surface, adding subtle patterns and texture - especially over large flat areas of paintwork, or it can be used to add linear interest by scratching fine lines into grass, fur, hair or fabric. Painting, whilst a serious pastime, should be both enjoyable and satisfying and much can be learnt by experimenting and trying out things that may or may not work. Always remember that nothing you will do is irreversible - it is always possible to paint over or scrape off any mistakes.

This painting of lilies was done on a 36x24in (92x61cm) primed cotton duck canvas using a no4 flat bristle and a ¼in (6mm) flat synthetic brush, a painting knife and a graphite pencil. The colours used were titanium white, Payne's grey, raw umber, burnt umber, burnt sienna, yellow ochre, cadmium yellow, cadmium red, alizarin crimson, ultramarine, cobalt blue, sap green, they were mixed using Liquin and turpentine. You will also need a sharp knife and a roll of masking tape.

MATERIALS AND EQUIPMENT

6mm flat/ no4 bristle, painting knife, pencil titanium white, Payne's grey, raw umber, burnt umber, burnt sienna, yellow ochre, cadmium yellow and red, alizarin crimson, ultramarine, cobalt blue, sap green

The Painting

1 The basic shapes and positions of the flowers, vase and table-cloth are established with a thin mixture of cobalt blue and Payne's grey mixed with plenty of turpentine; alternatively use acrylic paint mixed with plenty of water. Using a no4 flat bristle brush, work loosely and freely by holding the brush at the very tip of the handle. Pay particular attention to the perspective of the tablecloth squares as these are what give the picture depth.

2 With a range of dull green mixes made using sap green, yellow ochre, burnt umber and raw umber, cadmium yellow, titanium white and Payne's grey, begin establishing the colours and position of the leaves and stems using the underpainting as a guide.

3 Continue the process until all of the foliage is blocked in - leave the position of any flowers clear, as much as possible, of paint. This will allow any light colours, which will be applied next, to stay clean.

4 Titanium white is used to block in the lily flowers, and a little burnt sienna is added to give the blush of colour seen on the petals.

5 A neutral grey mixed from burnt sienna, ultramarine and white is used to block in the shadows on the vase. Titanium white is then brushed into the lighter side cutting in carefully around any leaves and shadows.

6 With burnt umber, raw sienna and white a brown mix establishes the overall background colour. This has the effect of visually pushing the flowers forward. Cut in carefully around the flowers and leaves trying to use confidant brushstrokes.

7 The paintwork on the flowers and leaves should now have stiffened sufficiently to overwork white on the flowers and shades of green on the foliage. Because the paint you are working into is still wet you will need to use light but confident strokes of the brush to float on a new layer of paint.

8 Cadmium red, mixed with a touch of alizarin crimson, provides the colour for the squares on the tablecloth. Then pure titanium white is brushed onto the white areas, add a little yellow ochre and rebrush over the vase.

9 With a palette knife work into the wet paint drawing and describing lines onto some of the leaves and flowers. The painting is then left to dry over night.

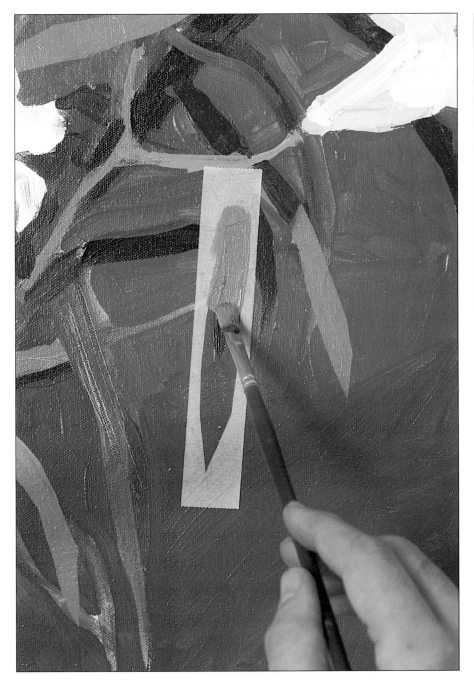

11 Work across the painting doing the same with all the flower petals, redrawing and reshaping them as you go.

10 When the paint has thoroughly dried, masking tape is used to redefine and consolidate some of the leaves; the tape is stuck to the canvas and the shape of the leaf cut with a sharp knife, be careful not to press so hard as to cut through the support. The leaf-shaped tape is peeled off and the area loosely blocked in with thick colour, the rest of the tape is then peeled off leaving a crisp leaf shape.

12 Mix a lighter background colour and with a ¼in (6mm) soft flat brush, scumble paint across the left hand side gradually tapering the colour off as it reaches the shadows. Put in a suggestion of light cutting through the foliage onto the wall on the lower right. Use a mixture of masking and straight brushwork.

13 Mask out areas of the pot and, using a soft graphite pencil, scribble on tone to give a suggestion of shadow.

14 Mask out the highlight area on the vase and block it in with pure white. Do the same with the tablecloth redefining the edge of the squares and the shadow cast by the vase.

15 The flower stamens are also cut from masking tape and brushed over with burnt sienna and cadmium yellow. The painting is finished by using the palette knife to pull unmixed cadmium red across the tablecloth suggesting the rise and fall of the creases in the material.

16 The finished painting.

Alternative Approaches

1 The wall behind this portrait of a writer and collector was cunningly made from corrugated cardboard. In order to paint it I placed strips of masking tape onto a large sheet of glass and cut them into thinner strips using a sharp scalpel, these were then used to mask out the wall before painting on the dark ochre.

2 Masking tape was also used on this picture of Tuscany, the trees and rows of vines were all masked with tape that had been cut or torn. The outline of the fields were made by painting over torn pieces of heavy watercolour paper.

THE GINGER CAT

Impasto and texture

OIL PAINT CAN BE applied to the support straight from the tube with little or no turpentine added; this gives a thick, deep, and very richly textured surface that holds the marks of the brush or knife and is known as impasto. The word impasto comes from the Italian meaning dough, and like dough the thick paint can be teased and manipulated to stand up in thick ridges that give a three-dimensional quality to the surface. This interesting technique is very expressive showing and preserving the direction and fluidity of the brush or knife strokes. This directional application of paint can be used to follow and describe the form of the subject but it does call for very sure handling and confident brush work.

Impasto is usually done alla prima or in the later and final stages of a painting that has been built and worked in thinner leaner layers. However it is possible to paint with scumbles and glazes over the top of impasto work to develop yet more dramatic , highly effective and interesting effects, however you must allow the impasto to dry before this is done, and that can take between several months to a year!

Impasto work is best done on a surface that has at least some tooth - on smooth surfaces the paint tends to slide when it is applied, so wooden panels should be roughened with coarse sandpaper or scraped over with a saw blade. You can, if you wish, even add marble dust or sand into the primer. You can also add sand, sawdust or plaster into the paint to give it more body and texture. Impasto media are available that bulk out the paint making it go further, and you'll need them! Even a moderately sized impasto painting can eat up your paint at an alarming rate. These media happily do not alter the colour of the paint but they do speed up the drying time. Take care if using these extender media with brushes as they will easily clog and spoil them.

This painting was done on a primed cotton duck canvas that measured 16x15in (41x38cm), charcoal was used for the underdrawing, three brushes were used - a no4 and a no8 flat bristle and a ¼in (6mm) flat synthetic, you will also need a painting knife. The colours used were titanium white, Payne's grey, raw umber, raw sienna, burnt sienna, yellow ochre, cadmium yellow, cadmium red, cadmium orange, cobalt blue and sap green; they were mixed using linseed oil and turpentine and little ordinary builder's sand.

MATERIALS AND EQUIPMENT

6mm flat/ no4 and 8 bristle, painting knife titanium white, Payne's grey, raw umber, raw sienna, burnt sienna, yellow ochre, cadmium yellow, red and orange, cobalt blue, sap green

The Painting

1 Sketch in the position of the cat in charcoal and fix with spray fixative. The cat almost fills the canvas and is allowed to disappear off to one side, this makes for a more interesting composition than if the cat were positioned fully on the canvas, filling it completely.

2 Mix a little cadmium orange and burnt sienna with plenty of turpentine and, using a no4 flat bristle brush, begin to block in the ginger mid tone pattern of the cat's fur.

3 Lighten the mix with yellow ochre and white and complete blocking in the cat's fur. Then using cerulean blue and Payne's grey establish the shadows around the cat. These have the effect of both anchoring it to the wall whilst at the same time giving it some form and dimension.

4 The dark background and shadows on the stone wall are painted using Payne's grey. Titanium white with a little Payne's grey and raw umber added are then mixed and the top of the wall established.

5 Using the ¼in (6mm) flat synthetic the mixes are thickened and the cat's eye established. Mixes of cadmium yellow, burnt sienna, raw umber and white give a range of tones and colour seen around the face and head.

6 With the no4 flat bristle the dark pattern on the fur is painted in using cadmium orange, raw sienna and a touch of cerulean blue. Make the brush marks follow in the same direction and at the same angle as the way the fur lies.

8 With a mix of titanium white, yellow ochre and a little cadmium yellow but using the no8 flat brush, the lightest fur is blocked in. Use short strokes with plenty of paint on the brush, adding less medium to the mix will make the paint thicker.

7 With the ¼in (6mm) brush the pads on the feet are painted next using a mixture of cadmium red, titanium white and a little dark fur colour. Change to the no4 brush and lighten the fur mix with more cadmium orange and raw sienna and continue working the pattern of the fur.

9 Fine lines to represent the cat's fur are made with a painting knife by scratching into and gently through the paint to reveal the light canvas beneath.

10 With a thick mixture of Payne's grey and sap green and using the no8 brush block in the dark background with short random strokes. Do not brush the paint out flat but allow it to keep its shape.

11 Mix a little builder's sand with titanium white, raw umber and a little Payne's grey and mix well. Then apply this to the stone wall with a painting knife, working carefully around the cat.

12 The finished painting.

Alternative Approaches

1 Here, the paint has been applied in a number of ways. Sand was incorporated into the light green paint on the distant Tuscan hillside and in the lower right field. A spattered area can be seen in the purple field and in the lower foreground sandpaper, hessian and coloured paper have been collaged on.

2 Interest and movement is added to the paint surface of this Venetian view with thick and heavy impasto work in the sky and sea.

FRUIT AND VEGETABLES

Using a painting knife

THE PAINTING knife can take some getting used to after the easy versatility of the brush. But with practice you will find that the knife is an extremely useful tool capable of a surprisingly wide range of marks. Oil paint and palette or painting knives are made for each other, the smooth buttery consistency and the long drying time means that the paint can be manipulated and worked at leisure without any fear of it drying or stiffening too quickly as would be the case with acrylics. Colour is mixed on the palette and transferred to the canvas using the knife or squeezed from the tube directly onto the canvas. The colour applied with a knife invariably looks brighter and denser than the same colour applied with the brush, but care needs to be taken not to overwork the paint or it will lose its clarity and strength.

When painting with a knife, what you take off is almost as important as what you trowel on, only so much colour can be built up and you will find that it takes much practice to float a pure colour over another wet colour without disturbing it. A minimum amount of colour should be applied in the first instance, this can always be scraped back to the support still leaving a strong colourful image onto which thicker paint can be worked. This thin image that merely colours the canvas or board, acts as the underpainting, establishing the image and covering the white ground. A legitimate alternative is loosely to block in with thin paint using a brush. This could either be oils with plenty of turpentine added or acrylic paint could be used.

The support needs to be a fairly heavy grade canvas or textured board as quite heavy pressure is sometimes used when the paint is smeared on and scraped off. On lighter canvasses this can make dents, it also makes the work more hesitant and difficult if there is too much give in the surface. Like brushes, painting knives come in many shapes and sizes each giving a distinctive range of marks; some are easier to use and more adaptable than others and it will not take long before you will develop your own preferences. Painting with a knife uses far more paint than painting with a brush so, as mentioned in project six, the paint can be bulked out or extended with a smooth impasto medium.

The painting was done on a primed cotton duck canvas that measured 18x24in (46x61cm) using titanium white, Payne's grey, cadmium yellow, lemon yellow, Naples yellow, cadmium red, cadmium orange, alizarin crimson, ultramarine, cobalt blue and sap green, mixed and thinned with Liquin and turpentine and Oleopasto, a gel extender used in all mixes. A no4 flat bristle brush was used for the underpainting, and a large and a small diamond-shaped painting knife for the overpainting.

MATERIALS AND EQUIPMENT

no4 flat bristle brush, large and small painting knives, titanium white, Payne's grey, cadmium yellow, red and orange, lemon yellow, Naples yellow, alizarin crimson, ultramarine, cobalt blue, sap green

The Painting

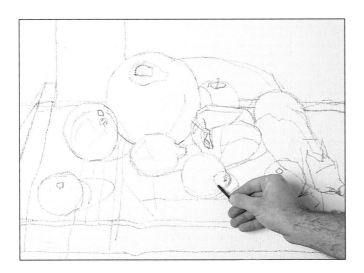

1 With a medium stick of charcoal draught out the composition onto the canvas.

2 Paint in the approximate colours, blocking in using thinned oil or acrylic paint. Don't pay too much attention to getting them correct. It is enough to paint the orange orange and the aubergine dark blue, the intention is to cover the support with an underpainting that gives a good ground on which to work and to lose some of the stark whiteness of the support.

3 Cadmium orange and cadmium red are mixed and, using a small diamond-shaped palette knife, begin to establish the overall colour of the squash. Lighten the mix with cadmium yellow and block in the orange - a little squash mix and cobalt blue give the dark colour for the shaded side. Work the paint by turning the knife into the shape of the object following its contours.

4 Turn your attention to the tomatoes. Darken the orange mix with cadmium red and use the small knife to block them in - as before move the knife around the form as if you are scraping its surface. The mix is darkened with alizarin crimson for the pepper and a little added white gives the shine on the skin.

5 Mix a mid green with sap green and lemon yellow, add a little white and block in the apple and the green pepper stalk. Add cobalt blue for the green on the aubergine stalk and white for the highlight.

6 Cadmium yellow, lemon yellow and titanium white give mixes for the lemons. Adding more white finds the highlight colour for the orange and the squash, this is dabbed on using the very tip of the small knife. The knife is also used to scrape into the squash, suggesting the patterns on its skin.

7 The dark colour of the aubergine is mixed with alizarin crimson, ultramarine and Payne's grey. The lighter reflection on the surface is made by adding white. Place a little of this dark aubergine colour beneath the other fruit to create the dark shadows.

8 Cobalt blue, cadmium red, Payne's grey and white mixes make up the shadows and creases on the tablecloth. Payne's grey is used for the dark patch seen in the background on the left hand side.

9 Naples yellow and titanium white are mixed and, using a larger diamond-shaped palette knife, the background is established.

10 For the tablecloth titanium white is applied straight from the tube. Work carefully around the shadows and the pattern, dabbing in the highlights at the end.

Alternative Approaches

1 The thick swirling paint describes perfectly the ripples of disturbed water around the swimmer. The light catching the paint surface also contributes to the illusion of wetness.

2 The thick smeared paint in this small palette knife sketch of the topiary garden at Levens Hall suits the sculptural qualities seen in the shaped yew and box trees and hedges.

PORTRAIT

Glazing

PROJECT EIGHT

GLAZING IS THE OLDEST of all oil painting techniques; a glaze is a thin transparent layer of paint which is applied over another layer of paint. Light passing through these transparent layers is reflected back by any opaque underpainting or ground giving the work a glow or inner light that is difficult to achieve by any other means. The traditional technique of glazing was executed over a grey tonal underpainting, or grisaille, which established the form of the subject and looked like a pale black and white photograph. The underpainting needs to be as light as possible whilst still showing the tonal range of the subject, this is because each layer or glaze of colour darkens the overall tone a little more. When two colours are glazed one on top of another in this traditional way, the resulting colour can be completely different than if the colours were mixed together wet in wet.

A painting does not have to be worked using only glazes, the technique can be used in tandem with other techniques and is especially effective when used over thick impasto work. The thin transparent colour settles more thickly in the troughs and crevices of the paint and less thickly on the peaks, making the intensity of the colour vary across the glazed area. Many artists use a glaze in the final stages of a painting, a carefully chosen colour glazed over the entire picture has a unifying and harmonising effect on the colours as a whole. Alternatively a glaze can be applied simply to darken the tone of a colour without remixing that colour to make it darker.

The way I have chosen to paint this self portrait uses the glazing technique in a slightly different way to the traditional approach but the principles are the same - each layer consolidates, modifies and qualifies the one beneath. Working on a white gessoed board the picture is painted using paint thinned with a quick drying glazing medium. Once dry the painting is completely recovered again using thin paint, the colours become darker and richer but still allow the work beneath to show through. Only two layers or paint glazes were used and the portrait will need several more before it is finished but already you will be able to detect the warm glow or light so characteristic of glazed paintings, that seems to emerge from beneath or within the paint work.

The portrait is painted on a 16x12in (41x30cm) piece of MDF (medium density fibre) board that has been prepared with four coats of acrylic gesso. The paint was mixed and thinned with a glazing medium and turpentine; the colours used were titanium white, Payne's grey, raw umber, burnt sienna, yellow ochre, cadmium red, ultramarine and cerulean blue. The drawing was done with a F pencil and three brushes were used, a ⅛in (3mm) and a ¼in (6mm) synthetic flat and a no8 bristle flat.

MATERIALS AND EQUIPMENT

3mm/6mm flat and no8 bristle brushes, grade F pencil, titanium white, Payne's grey, raw umber, burnt sienna, yellow ochre, cadmium red, ultramarine, cerulean blue

The Painting

1 With a F pencil the portrait is carefully drawn on a gessoed panel made from MDF. The board is hard and smooth so the pencil line stays crisp and fine, making it possible to indicate a fair amount of detail. Fix using a spray fixative.

2 With a synthetic ⅛in (3mm) flat brush, burnt sienna and Payne's grey are mixed with a little glazing medium, the shapes of the eyes are carefully painted and the dark shadow beneath the brow. A little cobalt blue and yellow ochre is added which makes a dull green for the iris, Payne's grey into the mix gives the pupil colour. Leave any highlights as bare gesso.

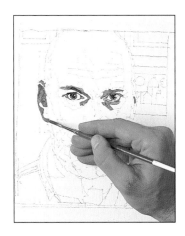

3 With cadmium red and raw umber work around the eyelids, add raw umber and establish the eyebrows. A little yellow ochre mixed with cadmium red gives the colour for the shadows beneath the eyes. The same colours are used in and around the ear.

4 Thin brown mixes of raw umber, Payne's grey and yellow ochre establishes the beard and hair, these are blocked in using the ¼in (6mm) flat brush. Work carefully to suggest individual strands of hair and work around as many lighter hairs as possible.

5 Cadmium red, yellow ochre and raw umber with a little added titanium white gives a darkish skin tone, this is used on and around the lips, nose and eyes, the creases on the forehead and in the shadow on the neck.

6 Lighten the mix with cadmium red and a little lemon yellow, ochre and white, thin with plenty of glazing medium and block in the mid tones over the left side of the face and neck.

7 Lighten the mix with white, add a little more glazing medium and block in the lighter tones on the opposite side of the face.

8 Lighten the mix further with a little more white and medium then paint in the highlights. Add a little grey and white into the mix and paint in the whites of the eyes. Raw umber and burnt sienna give the dark brown colour for the frames seen on the wall behind the head. The dark of the shirt is painted using the small ⅛in (3mm) brush and Payne's grey mixed with a little cerulean blue.

9 Using the ¼in (6mm) brush mix cerulean blue, Payne's grey and titanium white for the denim shirt. Lighten the mix with white for the highlights. White, Payne's grey and a little ochre is then mixed and used for the background wall.

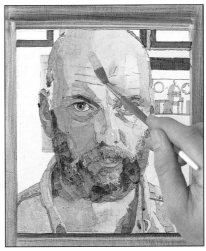

10 Payne's grey and raw umber are mixed and, using a no8 flat bristle and a ruler as a guide, paint in the mirror's wooden frame, the bristles on the brush leave lines suggesting wood grain. Then block in the background colour using yellow ochre, Payne's grey and titanium white. Once this first layer of paintwork is complete the painting is put to one side and allowed to dry thoroughly.

11 Once dry, which will take over night, the painting is reworked. The flesh tones are glazed over and modified using flesh tints similar to those used on the first coat, this consolidates and deepens the colour. If you come across areas of colour that you are happy with simply paint round them.

12 Details are repainted in and around the eyes cutting around the highlights which are made by the bare gessoed board showing through. The shadows are darkened and detail in the beard repainted.

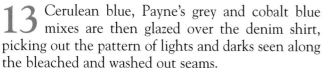

13 Cerulean blue, Payne's grey and cobalt blue mixes are then glazed over the denim shirt, picking out the pattern of lights and darks seen along the bleached and washed out seams.

14 Finally the background is recovered and the frame glazed using a dark brown made from raw umber, burnt sienna, and a little cadmium red. The painting will now be allowed to dry overnight and the process gone through again, this can continue layer after layer until the desired and satisfactory result is achieved.

Alternative Approaches

1 In this sketch for a larger painting of my daughter at Giza, the Sphinx and the pyramids have been built using thin layers of glazed paint. Done on gessoed hardboard the painting was originally without a figure, this was added later using thicker more opaque paint.

2 Four shades of blue were used to paint the water in this painting of Venice. Working over a light blue base colour the waves and ripples were glazed in layers the lightest first, the darkest last.

INDEX